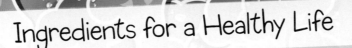

Ingredients for a Healthy Life

VERY TASTY VEGETABLE Recipes

Gareth Stevens
PUBLISHING

By Kristen Rajczak

Please visit our website, www.garethstevens.com. For a free color catalog of all our high-quality books, call toll free 1-800-542-2595 or fax 1-877-542-2596.

Library of Congress Cataloging-in-Publication Data

Rajczak, Kristen.
Very tasty vegetable recipes / by Kristen Rajczak.
  p. cm. — (Ingredients for a healthy life)
Includes index.
ISBN 978-1-4824-0576-7 (pbk.)
ISBN 978-1-4824-0578-1 (6-pack)
ISBN 978-1-4824-0575-0 (library binding)
1. Cooking (Vegetables) — Juvenile literature. 2. Vegetables — Juvenile literature. I. Rajczak, Kristen. II. Title.
TX401.R35 2014
641.6—dc23

First Edition

Published in 2015 by
Gareth Stevens Publishing
111 East 14th Street, Suite 349
New York, NY 10003

Copyright © 2015 Gareth Stevens Publishing

Designer: Andrea Davison-Bartolotta
Editor: Kristen Rajczak

Photo credits: Cover, pp. 1, 9, 11, 15, 17, 19, 21–24 (broccoli background) vic dd/Shutterstock.com; cover, pp. 1 (muffins), 15 (both) truembie/Shutterstock.com; cover, pp. 1 (frittata, soup), 4 (vegetables), 11, 14, 21 (arrows) iStockphoto/ Thinkstock; p. 4 (notebook) mexrix/Shutterstock.com; p. 5 Monkey Business Images/Shutterstock.com; p. 7 (beets) Jerry Rainey/Shutterstock.com; p. 7 (carrots) LiliGraphie/Shutterstock.com; p. 7 (asparagus) Zigzag Mountain Art/ Shutterstock.com; p. 7 (cabbage) Otmar Smit/Shutterstock.com; p. 7 (celery) Alfredo Maiquez/Shutterstock.com; p. 7 (garlic) clearimages/Shutterstock.com; p. 7 (cauliflower) ittipon/Shutterstock.com; p. 7 (spinach) kreatorex/ Shutterstock.com; p. 7 (radishes) ankiro/Shutterstock.com; p. 8 gillmar/Shutterstock.com; p. 9 studiogi/Shutterstock.com; p. 10 Africa Studio/Shutterstock.com; p. 12 Adisa/Shutterstock.com; p. 13 Jamie Grill/Getty Images; p. 17 (broccoli) nito/Shutterstock.com; p. 17 (peanuts) Dan Kosmayer/Shutterstock.com; p. 17 (red pepper) Volodymyr Goinyk/ Shutterstock.com; p. 18 Viktar Malyshchyts/Shutterstock.com; p. 19 Lukas Hejtman/Shutterstock.com; p. 20 Julian Watt/ The Image Bank/Getty Images; p. 21 (girl) michaeljung/Shutterstock.com.

Printed in the United States of America

CPSIA compliance information: Batch #CS15GS: For further information contact Gareth Stevens, New York, New York at 1-800-542-2595.

Contents

> ! Recipes in this book may use knives, mixers, and hot stove tops. Ask for an adult's help when using these tools.

Words in the glossary appear in **bold** type the first time they are used in the text.

Veggie Mania!

Vegetables come in all the colors of the rainbow, from the deep red of beets to the bright green of zucchini. The flavors and **textures** change from vegetable to vegetable, too. Green beans are sweet and crisp, while greens like kale can be chewy and a little bitter.

Lucky for us, all vegetables have lots of **nutrients**, so we can choose to eat our favorites most often. But don't forget to try new vegetables—eating many different kinds of veggies gives you the most health benefits!

Do You Have Allergies?

The **recipes** in this book may use **ingredients** that contain or have come into contact with nuts, gluten, dairy products, and other common causes of **allergies**. If you have any food allergies, please ask a parent or teacher for help when cooking and tasting!

Aim to fill half your plate with veggies at dinnertime and eat a vegetable or fruit with every snack and meal.

Vegetable Detective

Vegetables are the parts of plants that people can eat.

They're often put into five groups:

- root vegetables: beets, carrots, radishes, turnips

- stem vegetables: asparagus, kohlrabi

- leaf and leafstalk vegetables: cabbage, celery, lettuce, spinach

- bulb vegetables: garlic, onions

- head or flower vegetables: broccoli, cauliflower, artichokes

Some foods you may call vegetables are actually fruits. Eggplant, tomatoes, cucumbers, and squash are known as vegetables but are really fruits. They're considered vegetables because they're more often a dinner food than a dessert food, like strawberries might be.

CHEW ON THIS!

A fruit is a plant part grown to carry a plant's seeds.

These are only a few of the many vegetables you can include in your healthy **diet**!

7

Farm to Table

The fresh vegetables you find in the produce section of the grocery store are commonly grown on big farms. They've often traveled a great distance on refrigerated trucks to be placed in your cart and made for dinner.

Other vegetables are **preserved** soon after they're picked. They may be frozen or canned. As long as you choose frozen and canned vegetables that don't have a lot of added salt or creamy sauces, they're a healthy choice for a quick side dish.

CHEW ON THIS!

Pickles are made from cucumbers, but many veggies can be pickled, too. They're preserved by soaking in a salty liquid called brine for several weeks.

Very Veggie Soup

makes 4 servings

Ingredients:

1 tablespoon olive oil
1 onion
2 large carrots
1 stalk celery
1 cup green beans
1 zucchini
1/2 teaspoon salt
1/4 teaspoon black pepper
1/4 teaspoon oregano
2 cups chicken or vegetable stock
2 tablespoons tomato paste

Vegetable soup is easy to make! You can use whatever vegetables you have on hand, including frozen peas, canned tomatoes, or even spinach. Adding a can of garbanzo or black beans makes this a heartier meal.

Directions:

1. Chop the onion, carrots, celery, green beans, and zucchini, and put them into separate bowls.
2. Heat the olive oil in the bottom of a large pot on medium-low heat. Add the onion and stir for about 1 minute.
3. Add the chopped carrot and celery, and season with the salt, pepper, and oregano. Cook for about 3 minutes, stirring a few times.
4. Stir in the chopped zucchini and green beans. Cook together for about 1 minute.
5. Pour in the chicken or vegetable stock, and mix in the tomato paste. Bring it to a boil.
6. Lower the heat so the soup simmers for about 20 minutes, stirring a few times.

Creative Cooking

The key to eating enough vegetables is finding ways you like to eat them. Root vegetables taste great when they're roasted in the oven, similar to the sweet potato recipe on the next page.

Broccoli and sugar snap peas are delicious stir-fried or eaten raw with dip, such as hummus. If you don't like many vegetables, chop them up really small and add them to meatloaf or macaroni and cheese. This way, you're still getting important nutrients!

fresh vegetable salad

CHEW ON THIS!

A big, fresh salad is one easy way to get a few servings of veggies. Start with a bed of spinach or chopped romaine lettuce, and then add whatever veggies you have at home. Top with some shredded cheese, sunflower seeds, or avocado. Be creative, and use what you like!

Sweet Potato Fries

makes 4 servings

Ingredients:

2 medium sweet potatoes, cut into 1/2-inch wedges
3 tablespoons olive oil
1 teaspoon salt
1/2 tablespoon cinnamon

Directions:

1. Preheat oven to 350 degrees.
2. Put cut sweet potatoes in a big bowl. Pour olive oil over them and toss to coat.
3. Sprinkle the salt and cinnamon over the sweet potatoes. Toss again to get some on all the pieces.
4. Spray a cookie sheet with cooking spray. Spread the sweet potato wedges on the sheet in a single layer. You may need more than one cookie sheet.
5. Bake in the oven for 15 minutes. Turn the sweet potatoes over and return to the oven to bake for another 20 minutes.
6. Serve with ketchup, honey, or peanut butter for dipping!

Sweet potatoes are great for you—but they can be hard to cut up. Ask an adult for help using a sharp knife to make these. Then enjoy a healthy version of this popular side dish with your next meal!

Eat Up!

Vegetables are very important in your diet because they contain nutrients called vitamins and minerals. These are important to your body's function and growth.

NUTRIENT	WHAT IT DOES	WHAT TO EAT
vitamin A	keeps eyes healthy; supports the function of the heart, lungs, and other organs	sweet potatoes, spinach, carrots, summer squash
vitamin C	helps the body fight off illness and grow and repair	peppers, broccoli, Brussels sprouts, kale, potatoes
iron	makes up a part of blood that moves oxygen throughout the body	cooked spinach, Swiss chard, artichokes, beets
potassium	supports **cell**, muscle, and **nerve** health	tomatoes, cucumbers, eggplants, zucchini, pumpkins, potatoes
calcium	builds healthy bones and teeth	celery, cabbage, spring onions, spinach

Diets that include lots of vegetables and fruit have been shown to help lower blood pressure and keep your heart healthy.

Hot or Not

If you like spicy food, you're probably familiar with Tabasco sauce. But did you know that Tabasco is a kind of pepper? Along with cherry and cayenne peppers, Tabasco peppers are hot! Sweet peppers, or bell peppers, aren't hot at all. They're tasty sliced and added to stir-fries or eaten raw alongside other crisp vegetables, such as carrots and celery sticks.

No matter what kind of pepper you eat, they're all good for you. Peppers have lots of vitamins A, C, and K, with red bell peppers containing the most.

CHEW ON THIS!

Peppers are native to the Americas. They spread throughout Europe after 1493 when pepper seeds were taken to Spain.

hot peppers

Egg-cellent Veggie Frittata

makes 6 servings

Ingredients:

1 tablespoon olive oil
4 large eggs
2 cups of tightly packed fresh spinach, chopped
1 cup shredded cheddar cheese
1/4 cup red pepper, chopped
3 green onions, sliced
1/4 cup fresh tomato, diced
pinch of salt and pepper
fresh basil, chopped

Directions:

1. Preheat oven to 350 degrees.
2. In a pan on the stove top, heat the olive oil on medium heat. Add the pepper and onions. Cook for about 3 minutes, stirring a few times.
3. Transfer the pepper and onions to a bowl. Allow to cool.
4. In another bowl, use a fork or whisk to beat the eggs.
5. Add the cheese, spinach, tomatoes, beaten eggs, salt, and pepper to the cooked pepper and onions. Mix together.
6. Spray a pie plate with cooking spray. Pour the egg mixture into the pie plate.
7. Bake for about 40 minutes, or until a knife inserted in the center comes out clean. Serve slices with chopped basil on top.

Frittatas are an egg dish that can be made with many different combinations of cheese and vegetables. Don't like spinach? Try chopping up some broccoli and adding that instead!

Broccoli Power

People have eaten those little trees on your plate since the days of ancient Rome! There's a good reason for that. Broccoli is a nutrient powerhouse! It's full of antioxidants, which are nutrients that may lessen the risk of heart disease, eye problems, and **cancer**.

A little cooking brings out a sweet flavor in broccoli. Cut it up into bite-sized pieces and toss with olive oil and salt. Then, bake the broccoli in the oven on a cookie sheet for about 10 minutes.

CHEW ON THIS!

Like many fruits and vegetables, broccoli is a good source of fiber. Fiber is a nutrient that helps move food through your body and out as waste. It also keeps you feeling fuller, which is why vegetables help maintain a healthy weight.

Spicy, Nutty Broccoli Stir-Fry

Ingredients:

1/3 cup creamy natural peanut butter
1/2 cup water
2 tablespoons brown sugar
2 tablespoons reduced-sodium soy sauce
1 tablespoon rice vinegar
2 tablespoons canola oil
1 1/2 pounds broccoli crowns, trimmed and cut into 1-inch pieces
1 large red bell pepper, sliced
2 cloves garlic, minced
crushed red pepper flakes
1/4 cup chopped unsalted peanuts

Getting enough calcium and iron is important. Try this tasty broccoli recipe and take in a good dose of both!

broccoli

Directions:

1. Mix together the peanut butter, 1/4 cup water, brown sugar, vinegar, and 1 tablespoon of soy sauce in a bowl and set aside.

2. Heat oil in a large frying pan or **wok** on medium heat. Add the broccoli and allow to cook for about 5 minutes, stirring a few times.

3. Pour in the rest of the water and 1 tablespoon of soy sauce. Stir in the bell pepper and garlic, and cook with the broccoli for about 2 to 4 minutes, or until the water is gone.

4. Turn off the heat. Pour the peanut sauce over the broccoli and pepper and stir well.

5. Serve with a sprinkle of the chopped peanuts and crushed red pepper to each person's taste.

red pepper flakes

peanuts

17

More Than Pie

Thanksgiving wouldn't be the same without pumpkin pie! But pumpkin can be used for more than just desserts. Pumpkin, which is often sold as canned **puree** (pyuh-RAY), is a common ingredient in chili and sauces.

Still, if you prefer your pumpkin sweet, try mixing this vitamin C–rich food into vanilla yogurt with a sprinkle of cinnamon. Take in your daily vitamin A by topping a bowl of oatmeal with pumpkin. There are lots of ways to enjoy it!

pumpkin

CHEW ON THIS!

A great way to include more veggies in your diet is to mix purees into sauces, scrambled eggs, and baked goods. They add flavor and extra nutrients!

Pumped-Up Pumpkin Muffins

makes about 30 minimuffins

Ingredients:

1 1/2 cups white whole-wheat flour
3/4 cup sugar
1 teaspoon baking powder
1 teaspoon baking soda
pinch of salt
1 teaspoon pumpkin pie spice
1 can 100-percent pure pumpkin
2 eggs
1/2 cup canola oil or vegetable oil
1/3 cup low-fat Greek yogurt

These muffins have a lot going for them. Besides the healthy pumpkin in them, the whole-wheat flour and Greek yogurt will keep you full after you've had a couple of muffins for a snack!

Directions:

1. Preheat oven to 400 degrees.
2. Spray minimuffin tins with cooking spray.
3. Mix together the flour, sugar, baking powder, baking soda, pumpkin pie spice, and salt.
4. In a separate bowl, combine the pumpkin, eggs, oil, and yogurt.
5. Add the pumpkin mixture to the dry ingredients. Mix well.
6. Use a spoon to fill the muffin tins with batter.
7. Bake for 8 to 10 minutes, or until a toothpick inserted in the middle of one of the muffins comes out clean. Allow them to cool.

How Does Your Garden Grow?

Have you ever picked a juicy, red tomato right off the vine? There's nothing like eating foods you've grown yourself!

Planting your own vegetable garden is a fun way to help your family include more veggies in their diet. You can make the garden as big as you'd like—or just buy a small tomato plant to put on your porch. If you don't have a green thumb, you can still eat local vegetables by visiting a farmer's market in your town!

CHEW ON THIS!

For beginning gardeners, good foods to grow include carrots, peas, peppers, spinach, and tomatoes.

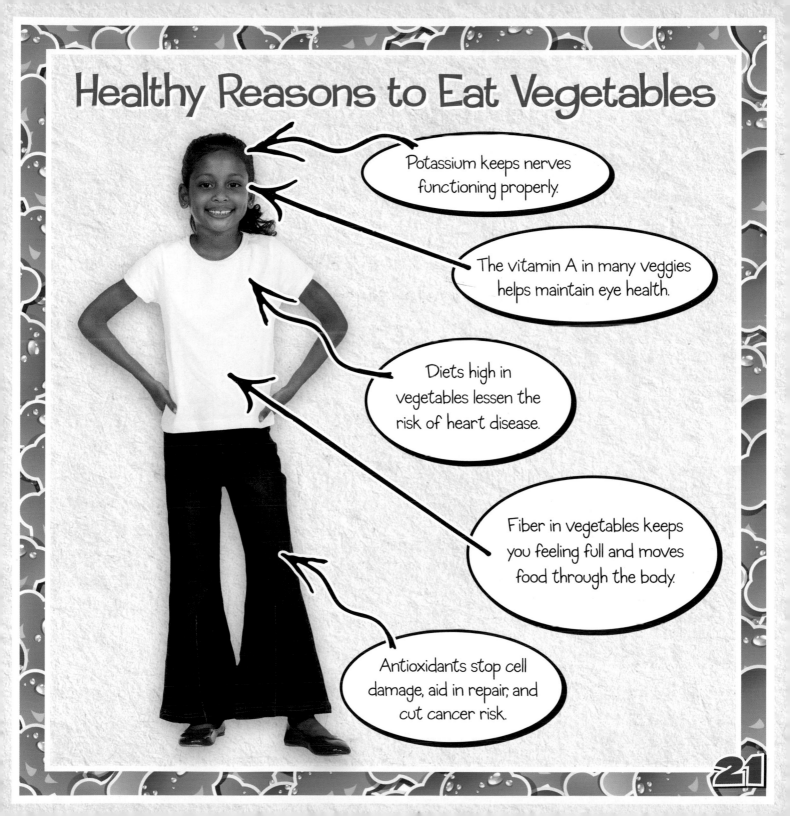

Glossary

allergy: a body's sensitivity to usually harmless things in the surroundings, such as dust, pollen, or mold

cancer: a disease caused by the uncontrolled growth of cells in the body

cell: the smallest basic part of a living thing

diet: the food one usually eats

ingredient: a food that is mixed with other foods

nerve: a part of the body that sends messages to the brain and allows us to feel things

nutrient: something a living thing needs to grow and stay alive

preserve: to keep something in an unspoiled state

puree: the paste or liquid created by grinding or blending cooked food

recipe: an explanation of how to make food

texture: the structure, feel, and appearance of something

wok: a large, thin metal pan with a curved bottom

For More Information

BOOKS

Falwell, Cathryn. *Rainbow Stew.* New York, NY: Lee & Low Books Inc., 2013.

Hengel, Katherine. *Cool Green Beans from Garden to Table: How to Plant, Grow, and Prepare Green Beans.* Minneapolis, MN: ABDO Publishing, 2012.

Tuminelly, Nancy. *Cool Fruit & Veggie Food Art: Easy Recipes That Make Food Fun to Eat!* Edina, MN: ABDO Publishing Company, 2011.

WEBSITES

Fruits and Vegetables
www.freshforkids.com.au/veg_pages/veg.html
Find out lots of information about many different kinds of vegetables!

Fruit and Veggie Color Champions
www.foodchamps.org
Play games, print coloring sheets, and learn all about fruits and vegetables.

Index